Virginia—
Thank you
for being
my friend!
Love,
paula

ZONDERKIDZ

The Blessings of Friendship Treasury
Copyright © 2014 by Mary Engelbreit Enterprises, Inc.
All rights reserved. www.maryengelbreit.com

Copyright© 1974, renewed 2002 EVIL EYE MUSIC, LLC. *Hug O' War*
reprinted with permission from the Estate of Shel Silverstein and
HarperCollins Children's Books.

This title is also available as a Zondervan ebook.
Visit www.zondervan.com/ebooks.

Requests for information should be addressed to:

Zonderkidz, 3900 *Sparks Dr., Grand Rapids, Michigan 49546*

Library of Congress Cataloging-in-Publication Data

[Blessings of friendship]
    The blessings of friendship treasury / [compiled and] illustrated by
    Mary Engelbreit.
        pages cm
    Originally published as: The blessings of friendship. Kansas City, MO :
    Andrews McMeel Pub., 2002. ISBN: 978-0-310-74509-9 (hardcover)
    — ISBN 978-0-310-74506-8 (epub) — ISBN 978-0-310-74495-5 (epub) —
    ISBN 978-0-310-74472-6 (epub)
        1. Friendship—Quotations, maxims, etc. I. Engelbreit, Mary, editor
    of compilation. II. Title.
    PN6084.F8B59   2014
    177'.62—dc23   2014004923

Editor: Barbara Herndon
Design: Cindy Davis

Printed in China

17 18 19 20 21 22 23 /DSC/ 15 14 13 12 11 10 9 8 7 6 5 4 3

For Laurie Lehman, Rena, and Christy!

−ME

AH! HOW GOOD IT FEELS THE HAND of an OLD FRIEND

LONGFELLOW

HUG O' WAR.

I will not play at tug o' war.
I'd rather play at hug o' war,
Where everyone hugs
Instead of tugs,
Where everyone giggles
And rolls on the rug,
Where everyone kisses,
And everyone grins,
And everyone cuddles,
And everyone wins.

—SHEL SILVERSTEIN

FRIENDSHIP NEEDS NO REASON!
·IBYCUS·

Smile

A smile costs nothing, but gives so much. It enriches those who receive, without making poorer those who give. It takes but a moment, but the memory of it sometimes lasts forever. None is so rich or mighty that he gets along without it and none is so poor but that he can be made rich by it. A smile creates happiness in the home, fosters goodwill in business and is the countersign of friendship. It brings rest to the weary, cheer to the discouraged, sunshine to the sad, and is nature's best antidote for trouble. Yet it cannot be bought, begged, borrowed or stolen for it is something that is of no value to anyone until it is given away. Some people are too tired to give you a smile; give them one of yours, as none needs a smile so much as he who has no more to give.

—AUTHOR UNKNOWN

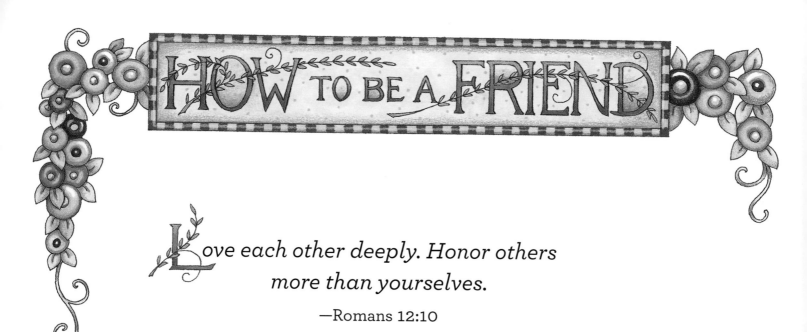

HOW TO BE A FRIEND

Love each other deeply. Honor others more than yourselves.

—Romans 12:10

A FRIEND LOVES
AT ALL TIMES.
SHE IS THERE TO HELP
WHEN TROUBLE COMES.

Do to others as you want them to do to you.

—Luke 6:31

LOVE ONE ANOTHER AND YOU WILL BE HAPPY, IT IS AS SIMPLE AND AS DIFFICULT AS THAT.

MICHAEL LEUNIG

WHEN YOU HELP SOMEONE UP A HILL, YOU GET THAT MUCH CLOSER TO THE TOP YOURSELF.

·ANONYMOUS·

The Helping Hand

If when climbing up life's ladder
You can reach a hand below,
Just to help the other fellow
Up another rung, or so,
It may be that in the future,
When you're growing weary, too,
You'll be glad to find there's someone
Who will lend a hand to you.

–AUTHOR UNKNOWN

riendship? Yes, please.

—Charles Dickens

Two people are better than one. They can help each other in everything they do.

—Ecclesiastes 4:9

We are each of us angels with only one wing; and we can only fly by embracing one another.

—Luciano de Crescenzo

There was a definite process by which one made people into friends; it involved talking to them and listening to them for hours at a time.
· REBECCA WEST ·

That's What Friends Are For

When life's being lived at a hurry-up pace
With hectic things happening all over the place,
A friend understands and allows us our space …
That's what friends are for.

When we're feeling grumpy and scowly and cross,
And not quite succeeding at being the boss,
A friend cheers us up so the day's not a loss …
That's what friends are for.

And when there's excitement and joy in the air,
Occasions to celebrate, good news to share,
There's one you can count on to always be there …
That's what friends are for.

They give us advice that we'd do well to heed,
Gently suggest the "fine tuning" we need,
Then join in our happiness when we succeed …
That's what friends are for.

We'll always be friends as we have from the start,
And when we're together or when we're apart,
Our friendship will always be close to my heart …
That's what friends are for.

—JAN MILLER GIRANDO

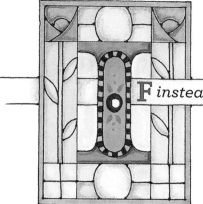

F instead of a gem, or even a flower, we should cast the gift of a loving thought into the heart of a friend, that would be giving as the angels give.
—George MacDonald

Think where man's glory most begins and ends, and say my glory was I had such FRIENDS.
—William Butler Yeats

HERE IS MY COMMAND. LOVE EACH OTHER, JUST AS I HAVE LOVED YOU.

—John 15:12

"From quiet homes and first beginning,
Out to the undiscovered ends,
There's nothing worth the wear of winning,
But laughter and the love of friends."

–HILAIRE BELLOC

A friend is the first one to come in when the whole world has gone out.

If I Could Catch a Rainbow

AUTHOR UNKNOWN

If I could catch a rainbow
I would do it just for you
And share with you its beauty
On the days you're feeling blue.

If I could build a mountain
You could call your very own
A place to find serenity
A place to be alone.

If I could take your troubles
I would toss them in the sea.
But all these things I'm finding
Are impossible for me.

I cannot build a mountain
Or catch a rainbow fair,
But let me be what I know best
A friend that's always there.

FRIENDS ARE THE FAMILY YOU CHOOSE FOR YOURSELF

· EDNA BUCHANAN ·

THE BEST THINGS IN LIFE... AREN'T THINGS

THE ONLY WAY TO HAVE A FRIEND IS TO BE ONE.

WHEREVER WE ARE, IT IS OUR FRIENDS WHO MAKE OUR WORLD.

ALL YOU NEED IS A FRIEND

When a sunny hello would help
brighten your day …
When you've just heard good news and
have volumes to say …
When two tickets turn up to a great matinee …
… all you need is a friend!

When the path that you're on turns surprisingly rough …
When wherever you're going, the going gets tough …
When you're giving your all but it's just not enough …
… all you need is a friend!

A friend speaks the truth when
it needs to be told …
Tells you you're radiant when
you feel old …
Gives you a nudge when
you must be cajoled …
Likes you as you are …

Joins in your mischief with
vigor and zest …
Makes you aware that you're
looking your best …
Leaves you alone if you
just need a rest …
But never strays too far.

When a role model's needed to keep you on track …
When you've tried to be open but don't have the knack …
When you've earned a good word and a pat on the back …
… all you need is a friend.

When it's shared, every day can be
even more fun …
And a duo is often much
better than one …
So remember each dawn as you
rise with the sun …
All you need is a friend!

—JAN MILLER GIRANDO

As I love nature, as I love singing birds,
and gleaming stubble, and flowing rivers,
and morning and evening, and summer and winter,
I love thee, my friend.

–HENRY DAVID THOREAU

ONE TOUCH of NATURE MAKES THE WHOLE WORLD KIN.

SHAKESPEARE

The Girls

Friendship never forgets.

That is the wonderful thing about it.
~ Oscar Wilde

THERE ARE PEOPLE WHO TAKE
THE HEART OUT OF YOU,
AND THERE ARE PEOPLE WHO PUT IT BACK.

— Elizabeth David

A friend is one of the nicest things you can have, and one of the best things you can be.
—Douglas Pagels

A friend is someone who reached for your hand and touched your heart.

*F*riends are kisses blown to us by angels.
—Author Unknown

A FRIEND IS SOMEONE WHO KNOWS ALL ABOUT YOU BUT LOVES YOU ANYWAY.

~ANON.

You are holy and dearly loved. So put on tender mercy and kindness as if they were your clothes.

Don't be proud. Be gentle and patient. Put up with each other. Forgive the things you are holding against one another. Forgive, just as the Lord forgave you. And over all of those good things put on love. Love holds them all together perfectly as if they were one.

—Colossians 3:12-14

MAKE NEW FRIENDS

Make new friends
but keep the old.
One is silver,
the other is gold.

A circle is round,
it does not end.
That's how long,
I will be your friend.

A fire burns bright,
it warms the heart.
We've been friends,
from the very start.

You have one hand,
I have the other.
Put them together,
we have each other.

Silver is precious,
gold is too.
I am precious,
and so are you.

You help me,
and I'll help you
and together
we will see it through.

The sky is blue,
the earth is green,
I can help
to keep it clean.

Across the land,
across the sea,
friends forever
we will always be.

—AUTHOR UNKNOWN

I'D LIKE TO BE THE SORT of FRIEND THAT YOU HAVE BEEN TO ME
I'D LIKE TO BE THE HELP THAT YOU'VE BEEN ALWAYS GLAD TO BE;
I'D LIKE TO MEAN AS MUCH TO YOU EACH MINUTE OF THE DAY
AS YOU HAVE MEANT, OLD FRIEND of MINE, TO ME ALONG THE WAY
· EDGAR A. GUEST ·